DATE DUE			
1/7-21			
2/26-22			
10/19			
9/25/00			
10/02/00			
1/07/02			

MINIBEASTS AS PETS

A TRUE BOOK

by
Elaine Landau

Children's Press®
A Division of Grolier Publishing

New York London Hong Kong Sydney
Danbury, Connecticut

Reading Consultant
Linda Cornwell
Learning Resource Consultant
Indiana Department
of Education

Author's Dedication:
For Jerry, Bianca,
and Abraham

Ladybugs on
a tree branch

Library of Congress Cataloging-in-Publication Data

Landau, Elaine.
    Minibeasts as pets / by Elaine Landau.
        p.   cm. — (A True book)
    Includes bibliographical references (p.) and index.
    Summary: Simply describes how to keep ladybugs, millipedes, crickets,
and ants as pets.
    ISBN 0–516–20388–6 (lib. bdg.)   0-516-26268-8 (pkb.)
    1. Insects as pets—Juvenile literature. 2. Millipedes as pets—Juvenile
literature. [1. Insects as pets. 2. Millipedes as pets. 3. Pets.] I. Title. II.
Series.
SF459.I5L35 1997
638'.5—dc21   97–17372
                                                                              CIP
                                                                              AC

Contents

Some people don't want minibeasts such as this millipede near them.

Minibeasts As Pets

You are surrounded by minibeasts. You've seen them on flowers, around trees, in meadows—and maybe even in your own house.

Some people don't want these creatures near them. But ants, ladybugs, crickets, millipedes, and other minibeasts can make fantastic pets!

Minibeasts are very small, so you don't need a large home or a yard to keep one. And these pets require far less care than ordinary pets, such as dogs and cats.

Minibeasts are very small, so you won't need much space to keep them.

You can probably find minibeasts around your home.

Minibeasts do not cost very much, either. Most of them cost nothing at all. You can catch them around your home.

Minibeasts provide their owners with a close-up view of nature. Many people never take the time to look at and learn about these fascinating animals.

Ladybugs

Just about everyone likes ladybugs. These brightly colored members of the beetle family are always welcome in a garden. That's because they eat insects that are harmful to plants.

There are several kinds of ladybugs. The ones you see

8

most often are red or orange with black spots.

Ladybugs make cute and unusual pets. On a warm, sunny day you can spot them in backyards, gardens, and parks. To capture ladybugs, let some crawl on your hand. Then gently place them in a plastic container with tiny air holes punched in the lid.

These creatures can live comfortably in a clear plastic container about the size of a shoe box, or in a large glass jar. A glass aquarium would also do nicely. Place some small plants inside the container to make it more like a ladybug's natural surroundings.

You can keep your ladybugs in a jar with a lightweight cloth over it.

Then stretch a lightweight cloth over the top to keep your pets from escaping. Every few days, carefully spray a little

A ladybug eats an aphid.

water into their home.
Ladybugs need moisture. They
also need light and warmth, so
place the container in an area
that receives a lot of sunlight.

Ladybugs like to eat small
insects called aphids. You can
find aphids on the stems and

leaves of many outdoor plants. Give your pets a fresh supply of aphids every day.

Enjoy your colorful little beetles. Let them crawl on your hand, but be gentle with them. An old legend says that harming a ladybug will bring you bad luck.

Enjoy your ladybug, and be gentle with it.

Beneficial Beetles

Even if most bugs give you the creeps, you probably like ladybugs. Everyone seems to like ladybugs. Everyone except aphids.

Aphids are tiny bugs that suck the juices out of plants. They will eventually kill the plants if they are not controlled. But ladybugs love to eat aphids. By eating aphids, they help keep gardens healthy. Because ladybugs are such helpful beetles, they are called "beneficials."

Millipedes

It's long and thin, but it's not a worm. It has lots of legs, but it's not a caterpillar. What is it? It's a millipede! Millipedes are wormlike animals—their long bodies are made up of many parts, or segments. They have two pairs of walking legs attached to most of their body segments.

16

Millipedes are long, wormlike creatures. They have two pairs of legs on most of their body segments.

There are between 7,500 and 10,000 kinds of millipedes throughout the world. They range in length from less than ⅛ inch (3 millimeters) to 11 inches (28 centimeters) long.

The most common millipedes in North America are brown and about 1 inch (2.5 cm) long. You can find them in damp places—underneath rocks and rotting logs or leaf piles.

Make a home for a pet millipede out of a plastic or glass container at least as large as a shoe box. Fill the bottom of the container with potting soil. (You can buy potting soil at a gardening center.) Add a few small rocks and some pieces

A container filled with soil makes a home for a millipede.

of tree bark. Millipedes need hiding places.

Your millipede needs a vegetable diet. Romaine lettuce, escarole, and summer squash are especially good choices. Also keep a small dish of water in your pet's container.

Millipedes may defend themselves by coiling up.

When frightened or attacked, millipedes defend themselves in two ways. They coil up into a ball, or give off a bad-smelling fluid. In a few types of milli-pedes, the fluid is poisonous.

The fluid is not harmful to humans unless it gets into an open cut or into your eyes or mouth. So be sure you always wash your hands after handling a millipede.

Always wash your hands after handling a millipede.

Ants

In some ways, ants are a lot like people. Just as we live together in neighborhoods, ants live in groups called colonies.

Also like people, ants have specific jobs to do. In an ant colony, there is at least one queen ant and many male

Ants live in groups
called colonies.

A queen ant

ants for the queen to mate with. There are also many worker ants that collect food and do other chores for the colony. You can keep ants in your own home. They are fascinating insects to watch.

Ants are easy to find during the warmer months of the year. Check for them under rocks and stones and near the base of trees. You can also

Ants are easy to find during the warmer months.

This mound of sandy soil is an anthill.

find them around an anthill— a mound of sandy soil that marks the entrance to an ant colony.

These minibeasts are quite small and fragile, so be especially careful when collecting them. Let a few climb onto a wooden ice cream stick. Then put them in a small plastic container or jar and carry them home.

Punch tiny air holes in the lid of the container so the ants can breathe. Be sure to make the holes very small and put the lid on tight—ants are outstanding escape artists!

You can make a more permanent home for your ants out of a larger plastic container or a glass aquarium. Place a layer of soil and stones in the bottom of your ant's new home. This will help to make it feel like their natural environment.

To keep your ants from escaping, cover their container with a piece of clear plastic wrap. As before, make tiny air holes in it.

These carpenter ants live in a system of tunnels they have chewed through wood.

An ant feasts
on an apple.

Ants are easy to feed. Just place small pieces of fruit and some hamburger or hot-dog scraps into their container. A tiny bit of honey spread over a stone is a special treat.

Use a magnifying glass to get a closer look at these insects. It's fascinating to watch them carry their food around and do other "chores."

Ants and Aphids

Ladybugs love to eat aphids. Ants love aphids too, but for a different reason. Aphids produce a sweet, sticky fluid called honeydew that forms tiny droplets on their backs. Ants like the taste of honeydew a lot.

An ant eats a drop of honeydew off the back of an aphid.

They wander through colonies of aphids and eat the honeydew off the aphids' backs. In return for the honeydew, ants protect the aphids from ladybugs and other insects that want to eat them.

Crickets

Crickets are jumping insects known for their songs. There are many kinds of crickets, but field crickets are the most familiar. They range in color from dark-brown to black. Both male and female field crickets have hearing organs, but only the males sing.

A male field cricket (above) and a female field cricket (left). Only the males sing.

You can collect field crickets in pastures and meadows. You can also find them along country roadsides.

A house cricket is sometimes called "the cricket on the hearth."

Another well-known cricket is the house cricket. These minibeasts look a lot like field crickets, but they are amber to light-brown. In the country-side, these crickets often find their way into barns, garages, and even houses. That's why this type of cricket is some-times called "the cricket on the hearth." If you live in the country, you may be able to capture one of these crickets without leaving your home!

If you cannot find any crick-ets in your area, you can probably buy both field and house crickets. Many bait and pet shops sell them as food for various animals.

Asian gift shops often sell small cages for pet insects. These tiny cages make good homes for crickets, but a plastic container is fine, too.

Small cages such as this one may be a cricket home.

Make sure the container has air holes so the crickets can breathe. Put an empty egg carton in the container with your new pets. The crickets will use it as a hiding place. If you provide them with enough food and water, they will usually settle down and not even try to escape.

Crickets eat green plants such as leaves and grass. They like fruit, too, but crickets need some additional

Crickets eat mostly
plant matter.

protein in their diet. You can provide this by giving them bits of leftover meat or small grasshoppers or aphids. Some cricket keepers prefer to feed their insects the mash sold at feed stores for young chicks.

Place a food dish in your cricket's home. Refill it as needed. Moisten some cotton balls with water and put them in a separate dish. Your cricket will drink from them.

Never fill the dish with water. A cricket can drown in even a small amount of water.

Crickets need a warm environment. The temperature of the room where they live should always be above 65° Fahrenheit (18° Celsius).

Many people believe it's good luck to keep a cricket. And it doesn't take much work on your part. So, good luck!

Some people believe crickets bring good luck.

To Find Out More

Here are some additional resources to help you learn more about minibeasts:

 **Books**

Bernhard, Emery. **Ladybug.** Holiday House, 1992.

Brenner, Barbara. **Where's That Insect?** Scholastic, 1993.

Demuth, Patricia. **Those Amazing Ants.** Macmillan, 1994.

Facklam, Howard. **Insects.** 21st Century Books, 1994.

Facklam, Margery. **The Big Bug Book.** Little Brown, 1994.

Godkin, Celia. **What About Ladybugs?** Sierra Club Books For Children, 1995.

Johnson, Sylvia. **Chirping Insects.** Lerner Publications, 1986.

Meyers, Susan. **Insect Zoo.** Lodestar Books. 1991.

Mound, L. A. **Amazing Insects.** Knopf, 1993.

Organizations and Online Sites

Acme Pet
http://www.acmepet.com/

Includes useful information on all kinds of animals.

American Society for the Prevention of Cruelty to Animals (ASPCA)
424 East 92nd Street
New York, NY 10128-6804
(212) 876-7700, ext. 4421
http://www.aspca.org/

This organization is dedicated to the prevention of cruelty to animals. They also provide advice and services for caring for all kinds of animals.

Iowa State Entomology Links
http://www.ent.iastate.edu/List/

Links to all kinds of sites about bugs.

Minibeast World Website
http://www.tesser.com/minibeast/

This site for young people offers lots of information about bugs. Created by the Young Entomologist Society.

Petstation
http://petstation.com/

An online service for pet owners and anyone interested in animals. Includes resources for kids.

Pet Talk
http://www.zmall.com/pet/

An online resource of animal care information.

Yahooligans Insect Links
http://www.yahooligans.com/Science_and_Oddities/Insects

This list of links to Web sites about insects is especially for kids.

Important Words

aphid a tiny insect that sucks juice out of plants

aquarium a tank in which fish, small animals, insects, or plants may be kept

beetles a large group of insects with biting mouthparts and hard front wings

escarole a leafy plant used in salads

hearth floor of a fireplace

mash a mixture of ingredients making up an animal's feed

moisture dampness

romaine a type of long-leaf lettuce

Index

Meet the Author

Elaine Landau worked as a newspaper reporter, children's book editor, and youth services librarian before becoming a full-time writer. She has written more than ninety books for young people.

Ms. Landau lives in Florida with her husband and son.